24.95

Provinces and Territories of Canada

# NEWFOUNDLAND AND LABRADOR

*— "A World of Difference" —*

Published by Weigl Educational Publishers Limited
6325 10 Street SE
Calgary, Alberta
T2H 2Z9

www.weigl.com

Library and Archives Canada Cataloguing in Publication data available upon request.
Fax 403-233-7769 for the attention of the Publishing Records department.

ISBN 978-1-55388-982-3 (hard cover)
ISBN 978-1-55388-995-3 (soft cover)

Printed in the United States of America
1 2 3 4 5 6 7 8 9 0  13 12 11 10 09

Editor: Heather C. Hudak
Design: Terry Paulhus

All of the Internet URLs given in the book were valid at the time of publication. However, due to the dynamic nature of the Internet, some
addresses may have changed, or sites may have ceased to exist since publication. While the author and publisher regret any inconvenience this
may cause readers, no responsibility for any such changes can be accepted by either the author or the publisher.

Every reasonable effort has been made to trace ownership and to obtain permission to reprint copyright material. The publishers would be
pleased to have any errors or omissions brought to their attention so that they may be corrected in subsequent printings.

Weigl acknowledges Getty Images as its primary image supplier for this title.
Government of Newfoundland & Labrador Dept of Mines & Energy: page 11 left; Innu Society of Newfoundland: page 24; National Archives of
Canada: page 25; Parks Canada: page 17 bottom.

We gratefully acknowledge the financial support of the Government of Canada through the Book Publishing Industry Development Program
(BPIDP) for our publishing activities.

# Contents

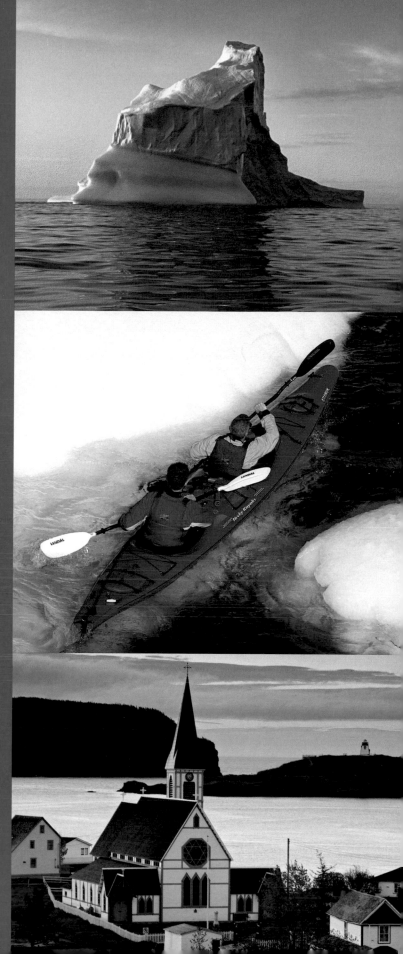

# Newfoundland and Labrador

Newfoundland, properly called Newfoundland and Labrador, is the easternmost province of Canada. It has two separate land masses— Newfoundland, which is an island, and Labrador, which is part of the Canadian mainland. Both the island and Labrador have long, rugged coastlines that have shaped the cultural, economic, and historical development of the province. The island of Newfoundland faces the Atlantic Ocean on its south and east coasts, and the Gulf of St. Lawrence on its west. The Strait of Belle Isle separates the island from mainland Labrador in the north, and the Cabot Strait separates it from Cape Breton Island to the southwest. Labrador has Quebec on all its borders but the east, where it looks out on the Atlantic Ocean.

The coastal city of St. John's is on the Avalon Peninsula. It began as a seasonal fishing outpost. Today, it is the bustling capital of Newfoundland and Labrador.

The island of Cape Spear, on the east coast of Newfoundland, is as far east as it is possible to go on the North American continent.

Newfoundland and Labrador are unique in appearance. In the Ice Age, glaciers thousands of feet thick covered the province. They scraped the soil off the rock below, deepened the river valleys, and rounded the mountains. When the glaciers retreated, they left hollows dug out by the ice. Thousands of shallow lakes and **bogs** were left in these hollows. The province's coastlines are cut by countless bays, inlets, and islands. Deep **fjords** are ice-filled for half the year, especially on the west coast and in northern Labrador. Both Newfoundland and Labrador have many rivers and lakes. The longest river is the Churchill, which flows from western Labrador into Lake Melville, the largest natural lake in the province. The river also boasts Churchill Falls. With a 75-metre drop, it is one of the greatest sources of **hydroelectricity** on the continent. In Newfoundland, the Exploits is the longest river. The Gander, the Humber, and the Terra Nova are other major rivers. The largest lakes on the island are the Gander, the Red Indian, and the Grand.

Newfoundland is Canada's youngest province, but it is one of the oldest settled regions in North America. Archaeologists and scholars have dated a site in Labrador to 5500 BC, and remains at Port aux Choix indicate that people lived there as early as 2340 BC. **Excavations** have also revealed that Vikings settled along Newfoundland's coastline in the year 1000.

Sheer cliffs make up much of Newfoundland's jagged coastline.

Newfoundland was claimed by Britain in the 16th century. Throughout the next few centuries, it remained a British colony. During World War II, army bases and military airports were built there. These bases became a major source of income for Newfoundland. The financial help the area had been receiving from Britain was no longer necessary. The economy flourished, and debates began over the future of Newfoundland. The decision to become a Canadian province was not an easy one. It took two separate votes before the issue was resolved. Newfoundlanders agreed to become Canadians by only 7,000 votes. The area joined **Confederation** on March 31, 1949.

**GET THE FACTS**

The puffin, sometimes called the sea parrot, is Newfoundland's provincial bird.

Newfoundland is about 525 kilometres from north to south, and 500 kilometres from east to west at its widest point. Labrador is more than twice as big as the island.

Gander airport is one of the first landfalls after the Atlantic Ocean.

There are some communities in Newfoundland that can only be reached by bush plane.

The ferry between Sydney and Port aux Basques is one of the largest in Canada. It features a video arcade and a movie theatre.

Lake Melville is connected to the ocean by a narrow inlet. The Smallwood Reservoir, which is twice as big as Lake Melville, is made up of hundreds of lakes that were united through a system of canals and dykes when the Churchill River was dammed.

# LAND AND CLIMATE

Newfoundland is made up of two regions—the Appalachian Region and the **Canadian Shield**. Southeastern Labrador and all of the island are part of the Appalachian Region. This land is mostly a plateau with parts that rise up to 610 metres high. There are also rugged hills, bogs, and small lakes in the flat, rolling plateaus of the south and east. North-central Newfoundland island is fairly flat, with gently rolling hills.

Most of Labrador is made up of the rocky plateaus of the Canadian Shield. It is a land of **tundra**, ice, and barren rock. In Northern Labrador, the Torngat Mountains dot the land. The highest point in Newfoundland is Mount Caubvick. It stands 1,622 metres above sea level.

Northern Labrador is a subarctic region—it has cool summers and cold winters. Average July temperatures reach only to about 13° Celsius, but they also drop as low as –51° Celsius. In January, the temperature usually sits at around –18° Celsius. The island's temperature is much more pleasant. July temperatures average 15° Celsius, and January temperatures drop to about –4° Celsius. However, winter temperatures can reach –34° Celsius throughout the season.

The sea around the Great Northern Peninsula is frozen from January until late May.

Foggy days are common in Newfoundland and Labrador. Warm weather systems moving up from the south clash with the cold sea currents. This causes an average of 124 days of fog each year in the eastern and southern coastal areas of the province.

Two national parks, 64 provincial parks, and several ecological and wilderness reserves help to preserve the natural habitats of the province's wildlife.

Winters in Newfoundland can get very snowy. Interior Labrador receives more than 450 centimetres of snow during the winter. Snowfall on the island of Newfoundland often exceeds 300 centimetres.

# NATURAL RESOURCES

Construction materials mined in the province include limestone, shale, sand, and gravel.

Newfoundland and Labrador have many mineral resources. Silver, gold, and nickel are a few of the many minerals hidden in the Canadian Shield of Labrador. Labrador also has rich deposits of iron-ore which account for a large portion of Newfoundland's mineral income. In 1994, large deposits of nickel, copper, and cobalt were found at Voisey's Bay. Gypsum, asbestos, and limestone are also mined on the island.

## KEEP CONNECTED

The Government of Newfoundland and Labrador Department of Natural Resources has a wealth of information on its website. Check it out at **www.nr.gov.nl.ca/nr**.

The Hibernia platform was built to withstand a collision with a one-million-tonne iceberg.

Buchans Mine mill complex overlooks the glory-hole pool, which is filled with water turned blue from oxidizing pyrite.

Among other important minerals in the province are the deposits of oil and natural gas that lie in the coastal waters. In 1959, engineers discovered the Hibernia fields off Newfoundland's coast. Huge petroleum deposits were found in this region.

GET THE FACTS

Buchans Mine, in central Newfoundland, produced more than 16 million tonnes of lead, zinc, copper, silver, and gold between 1928 and 1984.

About one percent of the province's land is farmed.

Newfoundland's lakes and rivers are a good source of power for driving hydroelectric generators. The province's first hydroelectric plants were built in the early 1900s.

# PLANTS AND ANIMALS

Gros Morne National Park is located in the southern part of the island of Newfoundland. It boasts beautiful landscapes and many types of animals.

The pitcher plant was named the provincial flower in 1954. It feeds off the insects that get caught inside its water-filled leaves.

Forests, mostly in the river valley, cover about one third of Newfoundland. White and black spruce, balsam fir, birch, and aspen trees grow in the province. Smaller plants, such as sheep laurel, blueberry, pigeonberry, and snakeberry, grow on the forest floor. Labrador tea, sundews, and pitcher plants flourish in marshy areas.

Some of Labrador's trees must struggle to grow in the poor soil and harsh climate. The ground is covered with common juniper, dwarf willow, and ground laurel. Reindeer moss and lichens are common in the barren lands. Only mosses and some low bushes can survive in the harsh northern tundra.

Black bears can be found throughout Newfoundland and Labrador. These bears can run as fast as 40 kilometres per hour when chasing prey.

Woodland caribou and black bears, as well as small mammals such as otters, beavers, muskrats, foxes, and lynxes, are found throughout the province. Wolves, porcupines, martens, and huge herds of caribou call Labrador home. Polar bears are native to the north coast.

Off the east coast, where the cold Labrador current mixes with the warm Gulf Stream, conditions are ideal for seals, whales, porpoises, dolphins, and many fish species. To preserve fish stocks, the federal government banned fishing for northern cod and other species in 1992. Their numbers were low, most likely from over fishing by people and by the seal population.

## KEEP CONNECTED

Information about wildlife living in Newfoundland and Labrador can be found at **www.newfoundlandlabrador.com/ WildlifeAndNature/Default.aspx**.

In mid-summer, fish called capelin thrive in the sea around Avalon. There are so many fish that people use nets and buckets to scoop them out of the water.

The Newfoundland dog is Newfoundland and Labrador's animal symbol. These dogs have thick, black coats that keep them warm during the province's cold winters and rainy seasons.

Three hundred different species of birds nest on the Newfoundland shore. Many kinds of ducks and geese live in the province during the summer. Millions of gulls, gannets, murres, kittiwakes, and puffins nest around the coasts. Sanctuaries have been set up to protect them.

GET THE FACTS

Moose were introduced to the island of Newfoundland in 1878. They are now so numerous that drivers are warned not to drive at night for fear of hitting one.

The black spruce is Newfoundland's provincial tree.

About 800 bald eagles frequent the Newfoundland area.

Ten thousand wild Newfoundland ponies once roamed the island. Today, only 269 ponies remain.

The most southerly caribou herd in the world lives on Newfoundland's Avalon Peninsula.

# TOURISM

ourism is a rapidly growing industry in Newfoundland. Visitors come from all over the world to see the province's rugged beauty and fascinating history.

St. John's is the oldest North American city north of Mexico. At St. John's Signal Hill National Historic Site, visitors are treated to a wonderful view of the town, the coast, and the port. For tourists interested in history, the Queen's Battery is a popular attraction. It is a fort from the time of the Napoleonic Wars. Today, actors reenact the English and French battles of the 1800s.

The Newfoundland Museum is also in St. John's. There, visitors get the chance to learn more about the province's history. Some exhibits are devoted to the lives of its Aboriginal Peoples, while others demonstrate the lifestyles of 19th-century settlers. Many tourists head to the northern tip of Newfoundland to explore the L'Anse aux Meadows National Historic Site. The Viking settlement at L'Anse aux Meadows dates back to the year 1000, and is the only known Viking settlement in North America. Visitors can walk among the reconstructed sod houses and learn how they were built.

Salvage Harbour is a fishing village near Terra Nova National Park.

Icebergs can be seen in the coastal waters near St. Anthony's.

In the spring and summer, icebergs of all sizes float down the coast of Labrador. Coastal boats carry tourists up the so-called Iceberg Alley, stopping at remote communities to watch for whales and icebergs.

L'Anse aux Meadows is the earliest known European settlement in the New World. Exhibits at the site highlight Viking lifestyle, artifacts, and various archaeological discoveries.

Maintaining the enormous generators that make up the Churchill Falls power station is a big job. Engineers work hard to keep the machinery running properly.

## KEEP CONNECTED

For more information about Churchill Falls, visit **www.heritage.nf.ca/law/cfimpacts.html**.

The economy of Newfoundland and Labrador is quite dependent on natural resources. One of Newfoundland's most important industries is fishing. Salmon, turbot, halibut, and flounder swim in the coastal waters. A ban on cod fishing in 1992 hit many fishing communities hard, but it also helped rebuild the stocks, and limited cod fishing is now allowed. In the 1990s, there were more than 500,000 tonnes of fish caught each year. This added about $250 million to the economy.

Forestry and mining are other important industries in the province. About two-thirds of Newfoundland's harvested wood is used to make newsprint. Newfoundland wood is also made into lumber and timber products.

Labrador's vast resources of iron ore are a major part of the province's mining industry. Iron ore mining accounts for about 90 percent of the province's mining income. About one half of the nation's supply comes from Labrador.

Lobster, crab, and shrimp are very valuable Newfoundland products, but they provide little employment. Catches are small, and they do not require much processing.

Hydroelectric power is a critical product. Newfoundland's Churchill Falls has 11 generators that use the power of falling water to produce electricity. People in Newfoundland only need about 29 percent of the total electricity generated by the falls. The rest is exported, mostly to Quebec.

# GET THE FACTS

Newfoundland is the country's leading producer of iron ore. Most iron is mined in the Wabush Lake region.

Unemployment in the province is high, but the future looks bright thanks to the mining and tourism industries.

For a long time, dried and salted cod was the province's main export. Today, frozen fish is a very important export.

Mining in Newfoundland and Labrador contributes about $1 billion to the province's economy. More than 3,000 Newfoundlanders work in the mining industry.

# GOODS AND SERVICES

The high cost of importing grain to Newfoundland has created a need for more local growers.

The production of milk in Newfoundland and Labrador has quadrupled in the last 20 years. The dairy industry now produces enough milk to supply the whole province.

**A**gricultural goods are important to Newfoundland's economy. Farm products bring in about $75 million each year. Since the province has a difficult climate and uncooperative soil, farmers must grow crops that will survive under poor conditions. Potatoes, turnips, cabbage, carrots, and beets are the most important vegetable crops produced in the province. Farmers have expanded their scope to include broccoli, cauliflower, and lettuce. Wild blueberries are abundant, and they are exported to other provinces.

Dairy products make up about one-third of the province's total agricultural industry. Newfoundland exports milk to other provinces, and the dairy industry creates about $27 million for the economy. Dairy cows and chickens are the most important animals in the province. Other livestock in Newfoundland include goats, beef cattle, and pigs. Animal farming provides hundreds of jobs both on farms and in processing and distribution.

Memorial is Newfoundland's only university. Its main campus is in St. John's.

**KEEP CONNECTED**

Information about Memorial University can be found by visiting **www.mun.ca**.

Newfoundland's main manufactured goods include processed fish and newsprint. Manufacturing in the province has had to overcome the small market size, the distance to other markets, and the shortage of skilled workers. Most factories in Newfoundland are located around St. John's. These factories manufacture goods such as food, paint, and fishing equipment. There are also small sawmills, seafood canneries, and brickyards.

About three-quarters of Newfoundland's employees work in the service industry. Service jobs include those in hotels and restaurants, airports, transportation, and government. Doctors are also in the service industry. Most health services in the province are free, and the province is combining hospitals to provide better service and economy.

The fishing industry employs fishers, as well as people to work in processing and sales.

Every two or three weeks, a government medical team flies in to Newfoundland outposts by helicopter to see patients and dispense medications.

Some villages in the province can only be reached by water. These communities often have their groceries and other essentials brought in by boats.

Vegetables including mushrooms, onions, peas, peppers, beans, and corn are now being grown and marketed in the province.

St. John's Water Street is the oldest street in North America.

The province has two daily newspapers, the *The Telegram* in St. John's and *The Western Star*. It also has several regional weekly newspapers.

Dogsleds were once used for winter travel in the northern part of the province. They have now been largely replaced by snowmobiles.

# FIRST NATIONS

When the first Europeans arrived, there were a number of Aboriginal groups living throughout the Labrador and Newfoundland regions. A group called the Innu lived in central Labrador and on parts of the Labrador coast. The Innu were nomadic hunters of large animals such as caribou. North of the Innu lived the Inuit. Like the Innu, the Inuit hunted caribou and moved from camp to camp. The Inuit are distantly related to the Dorset. The Dorset lived in Newfoundland from 500 BC to 1500 AD. They hunted sea mammals such as arctic whales and walruses.

Despite the threats of industrial development, logging, and social pressure, the Innu still practise their traditional ways of life through hunting, fishing, and food gathering.

It is commonly believed that the Beothuk were the first Aboriginal Peoples encountered by Viking explorers when they arrived on the island of Newfoundland. The Beothuk lived in small, conical **wigwams** in the summer. They hunted, fished, and collected eggs and shellfish. In winter, they lived in large log structures lined with moss to keep out the cold. During the spring and fall migrations, the Beothuk forced caribou, their main meat source, to cross rivers at certain points and killed them from their canoes.

When the Mi'kmaq migrated to Newfoundland from Nova Scotia, they lived peacefully with the Beothuk until around 1770. Then, other settlers encouraged the Mi'kmaq to attack the Beothuk. It was these attacks, along with the arrival of more European settlers and diseases, that led the Beothuk to eventually die out.

It is believed that a woman named Shawnandithit was the last Beothuk. She died of tuberculosis in June 1829, at the age of 28. She was able to give valuable information about her culture and language.

Inuit elders show younger generations how to make traditional items, such as sealskin kamiks. Kamiks are boots that protect the feet from extreme cold conditions.

The Norse are people from ancient Scandinavia. Norse Vikings are North America's first known European settlers. Knowledge of the areas that Vikings visited in North America is limited mostly to legends.

## KEEP CONNECTED

Learn more about the Vikings in Newfoundland at
**www.wordplay.com/tourism/viking.html**.

Vikings were probably the first Europeans to explore the shores of Newfoundland. Around the year 1000, Norse explorer Leif Ericson made several voyages west and southwest from Greenland. The discovery of nine Viking buildings near L'Anse aux Meadows shows that either Ericson or some other Norse explorer established a temporary settlement there. The Vikings may have stayed in the area for about 20 years, but abandoned it after attacks by local Aboriginal Peoples.

Five hundred years later, Portuguese and English explorers looking for the **Northwest Passage** to the Orient probably touched on the Newfoundland coast. In 1497, a navigator called John Cabot made the first of two trips to the Newfoundland area on behalf of King Henry VII of England. Cabot reported that there were so many cod, he could scoop them up in baskets off the side of his ship. Many European explorers followed Cabot, and the slow settlement of a "new founde lande" began.

Gaspar Côrte-Real, a Portuguese explorer, spent the summer of 1500 exploring Newfoundland. He named many of the bays and inlets in the area.

During his two voyages in 1534 and 1536, Jacques Cartier sailed through the Strait of Belle Isle and the Cabot Strait, proving that Newfoundland was an island.

An English explorer called Sir Humphrey Gilbert claimed Newfoundland for England in 1583. It became England's first possession in North America.

# EARLY SETTLERS

Newfoundland was not officially recognized as a British colony until 1824, more than 300 years after Cabot first visited the area.

The fishing stage operations set up by merchants started out as seasonal settlements that were built close to fishing sites. These processing facilities eventually grew into permanent settlements.

For almost a century after Cabot explored Newfoundland, fishers and whalers came to the province. Fishing boats from England, France, Spain, and Portugal arrived in Newfoundland waters. These fishers would haul in enormous catches of cod every summer. In 1583, despite the presence of fishing boats from many European countries, Sir Humphrey Gilbert claimed the Newfoundland territory for England.

Soon after Newfoundland was claimed, England's West Country Merchants were granted a **charter** that allowed them to establish colonies in Newfoundland. It also gave them exclusive rights to the area's offshore fishing grounds. The West Country Merchants did not want other permanent settlers in Newfoundland. They believed that settlers would compete with their profitable fishing fleets. The merchants went to great lengths to keep permanent settlers out.

During his explorations of Newfoundland, John Guy is said to have come in contact with the Beothuk in Trinity Bay.

In 1610, an English merchant by the name of John Guy brought thirty-nine settlers to Conception Bay. Guy and his settlers built a small community called Cupers Cove. By 1621, other settlements had been built at Cambriol, Renews, and Ferryland. These settlements were not successful. The harsh climate, poor soil, unprepared settlers, and threats from the West Country Merchants all contributed to the lack of success in settling.

Most outposts in Newfoundland had churches. Ministers would come in every few weeks on the coastal boats.

Small settlements were established throughout the 18<sup>th</sup> century, but complaints about the brutality of the fishing **admirals** continued to reach Britain. In 1729, the British Crown appointed a naval officer to govern the island. This appointment brought some order to Newfoundland, and the settlement rate began to increase.

Once the territorial wars between Britain and other European countries came to an end, English and Irish settlers arrived more consistently. A great wave of immigration occurred during the early 1800s, when the British government made it legal for colonists to own land and build homes. By 1827, more than 60,000 people occupied Newfoundland.

Around 1610, a pirate called Peter Easton lived in Harbour Grace and raided many villages on the coast.

In 1752, Governor Sir Hugh Palliser encouraged **Moravian** missionaries to come to northern Labrador. The Inuit were attacking English fishers along the coast, and Palliser hoped the Moravians could keep the Inuit inland.

A man named Dr. Wilfred Grenfell came to the Newfoundland area on a hospital ship sent by the Board of the Deep Sea Missions. He helped to raise money for hospitals, doctors, nurses, and boarding schools.

Irish settlers were often badly treated. One governor even tried to send them all home.

The admirals of the West Country Merchants discouraged settlers in the cruelest ways, with house burnings, whippings, and even hangings.

The islands of St. Pierre and Miquelon, just off the Burin Peninsula, actually belong to France.

Most of the province's early people settled in the bays and inlets of the east coast because fishing was so important and the soil was poor for farming. The first large population centre grew in St. John's and around nearby Conception Bay. Almost one third of Newfoundlanders still live in this area. Later settlement moved to the east and south coasts of the province.

Today, natural resources continue to draw people to certain areas of the province. The iron-mining town of Wabash Lake makes up about two-fifths of Labrador's population. Other mining centres and pulp-and-paper-mill towns gave rise to a larger inland population. Defence bases in St. John's, Gander, Stephenville, Argentia, and Goose Bay created other population growth spurts in the province.

About one-fifth of the people in Newfoundland and Labrador live in St. John's.

Most Newfoundlanders live along the coast. About 58 percent of the population live in urban areas, while the rest live on farms and in small logging, mining, and fishing villages. The number of people living in Newfoundland has decreased over the past decade. Due to economic hard times, many people have had to move to other provinces to make a living.

GET THE FACTS

Acadians were early French-speaking settlers. Today, many Acadians live on the west coast of Newfoundland.

Newfoundland and Labrador has a population of about 541,000, making it the second smallest province in terms of population.

Only Prince Edward Island has fewer people.

After St. John's, Corner Brook is the largest city in the province.

About 30,000 people live in Labrador. Labrador City is its largest community.

# POLITICS AND GOVERNMENT

St. John's has been the political centre of Newfoundland since 1818, when permanent civil governors were appointed by the British monarchy.

The House of Assembly of Newfoundland has 52 elected members. The leader of the majority party usually becomes the premier and appoints a cabinet of 16 ministers. The cabinet decides on government policies, and the ministers make sure their departments carry these policies out. The crown is represented by the lieutenant governor, who performs ceremonial duties and signs bills into law. The government funds services including major works projects, health services, education, policing, and highways.

Newfoundland has three cities and nearly 400 towns and communities. Major areas in the province provide municipal services for residents, but many of the coastal communities are too small or isolated to support a local government. Some of these communities do not collect taxes, enforce building codes, maintain roads, or even light their streets.

Newfoundland was the last province to join Confederation. The signing of the documents was carried out by the first premier of Newfoundland, Joseph Smallwood.

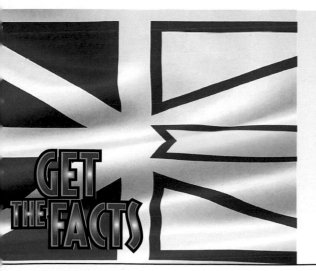

GET THE FACTS

Newfoundland's flag has four colours. White represents snow, red represents human effort, blue shows the importance of the sea, and gold celebrates a bright future.

Newfoundland is represented in Ottawa by six senators and seven members of Parliament.

Newfoundland's three official cities are St. John's, Corner Brook, and Mount Pearl.

There are two major political parties in Newfoundland and Labrador—the Liberals and the Progressive Conservatives.

Newfoundland's government and corporations actively support budding artists.

The provincial motto is *Quaerite prime regnum dei* which means "Seek ye first the Kingdom of God."

# CULTURAL GROUPS

Newfoundland's citizens are mainly descendents of settlers from southwestern England, southern Ireland, and Scotland. About 96 percent of the population speak English, and about 4 percent are bilingual, usually with French as the second language.

The province's people are different in many ways from other Canadians because they have been isolated for so long. One of the distinctive features is their manner of speaking. They have retained and modified the words and accents of their European ancestors. Many of the common words and phrases in Newfoundland are not so common in the rest of Canada. For example, Newfoundlanders call a small tin cup a "bannikin," a tourist is called a "come-from-away," and a pancake is called a "gandy."

Newfoundlanders are proud of their strong heritage and work hard to keep it alive. The Southern Newfoundland Seamen's Museum has exhibits of five centuries of sea-faring life at Grand Bank. Other sea-faring exhibits can be found throughout the province, and various historical sites preserve and explain Newfoundland's past.

Irish immigrants left Ireland for the English colony of Newfoundland to find work at the various fisheries.

The custom of **mummering** is popular in Newfoundland. It dates back to early settlers. Mummers, who consist of both professional actors and everyday people, dress in costumes and perform traditional folk plays. They also parade through the streets. During the 12 days of Christmas, mummers go from house to house in their costumes and disguises. They try to fool their hosts who, in turn, must unmask their visitors by guessing their identity.

There are two Innu communities in Labrador. The Sheshatshiu community pictured here is located on the shores of Lake Melville, and the Utshimassits community is on an island on Labrador's north coast.

Newfoundland's Aboriginal communities are also active in preserving and celebrating their cultures. A beach festival, held every July on Lake Melville, showcases aspects of Innu art and culture such as Innu tea dolls, hand-made moccasins, and wood and bone carvings. People at the festival also enjoy traditional Innu foods. The Labrador Inuit Association and the Torngâsok Cultural Centre work to protect Inuit language and culture for future generations. They help with education and give advice on understanding hunting regulations and land claims.

GET THE FACTS

The days when sled dogs were important are remembered in the Labrador 400. This international dogsled race lasts up to seven days. It starts and finishes in Labrador City.

Mummering is a significant part of Newfoundland culture.

A reserve on the Conne River on the south coast of Newfoundland was established for the Mi'kmaq in 1986.

Newfoundland has some very unusual place names, such as Come By Chance, Joe Batt's Arm, and Bacon Cove.

At Red Bay National Historic Site, archaeologists have uncovered a sixteenth-century whaling station.

Conne River Mi'kmaq Performance Choir celebrates Aboriginal traditions through song and dance.

# ARTS AND ENTERTAINMENT

**N**ewfoundland is far from the centres of mainstream Canadian music, art, and entertainment. As a result, most artists perform traditional songs, dances, and stories from the local area. More recently, new songs have been written about Newfoundland life and the sea. Newfoundland music often includes elements from Aboriginal music. Musicians play instruments that were played by their Scottish and Irish ancestors, such as the fiddle and the accordion.

The Newfoundland music scene is gaining recognition outside the province. Professional performers, including Great Big Sea and Kim Stockwood, have become well known in Canada and the rest of the world. The annual Newfoundland and Labrador Folk Festival, at Bannerman Park in St. John's, attracts folk singers, musicians, and storytellers from Canada, the United States, and Europe. The festival helps preserve the cultural traditions of the province through music, dance, and crafts.

*This Hour Has 22 Minutes* is one of Canada's most popular television programs. Cast members have included **Cathy Jones**, **Rick Mercer**, **Greg Thomey**, and Mary Walsh.

Newfoundland has also produced talented performers and writers. Cast members of the comedy show *This Hour has 22 Minutes*—Rick Mercer, Mary Walsh, Cathy Jones, and Greg Thomey—are all **Gemini Award** winners who have had success in radio, film, and writing. Nationally-known writer and commentator Rex Murphy was born just outside St. John's. Actor and writer Gordon Pinsent is from Grand Falls, Labrador and has found great success with his Newfoundland stories.

Newfoundland books and theatre productions are often drawn from folklore and tradition. Some are based on the lonely life of the outposts, as in the works of novelists Margaret Daley, Wayne Johnston, and poet E.J. Pratt. Bernice Morgan was born in St. John's. She has written many excellent novels, including *Random Passage*, which has sold more than 10,000 copies nation wide.

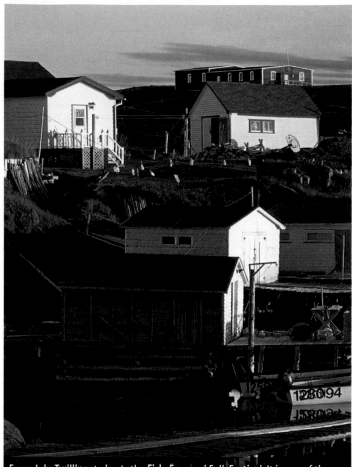

Every July, Twillingate hosts the Fish, Fun, and Folk Festival. It is one of the largest folk festivals in Newfoundland and Labrador.

GET THE FACTS

Great Big Sea is known throughout Canada for its energetic performances and lively folk rock.

Painters such as David Blackwood and Christopher and Mary Pratt have concentrated on Newfoundland's magnificent scenery and the objects of everyday life. Much of this art is associated with the sea.

The St. John's Arts and Cultural Centre presents the best Newfoundland entertainment from Canada and the world.

The Newfoundland and Labrador Drama Festival is held each April in a different location. It features storytelling, theatre, and dance performances.

The Gros Morne Theatre Festival takes place every summer in Gros Morne National Park. The festival consists of an assortment of plays and concerts, and features some of the finest actors from across the country.

The sea is the inspiration for many great Newfoundland songs.

Many communities in Newfoundland and Labrador fight the winter chill by holding carnivals. Parades, dogsled races, snow sculpting, skiing, and skating parties are all a part of the fun.

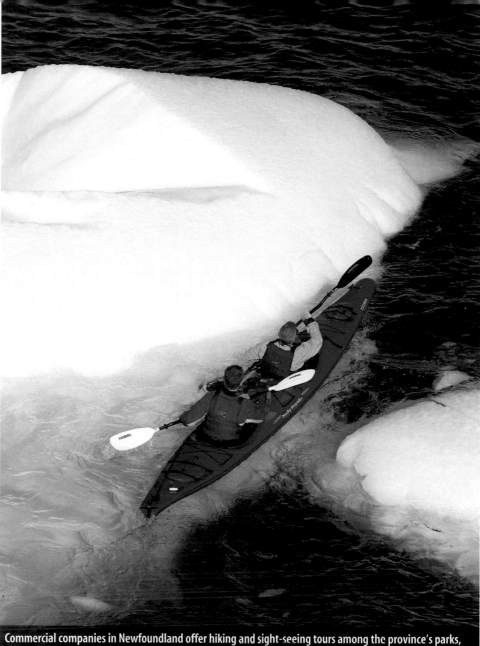

Commercial companies in Newfoundland offer hiking and sight-seeing tours among the province's parks, and whale-watching expeditions along the coast.

Many professional athletes get their start in Newfoundland and Labrador. The province has sent a number of players to the National Hockey League, including John Slaney from St. John's and Dan Cleary from Carbonear.

Most of the sport in Newfoundland and Labrador is at the amateur level and takes advantage of the countryside, lakes, and sea. Many North Americans have enjoyed hunting in the woods and fishing on the bountiful waters of the province. Kayaking and canoeing are also popular water sports.

Marble Mountain, a popular ski resort near Corner Brook, boasts the best ski hill east of the Rocky Mountains.

Most people in Labrador, and many on the island, own a snowmobile. Snowmobiling is a popular sport. It is also an excellent way of getting around when the land is frozen. The winter brings plenty of snowfall to the high land of Labrador and western Newfoundland. Downhill skiing, particularly at Marble Mountain near Corner Brook, is among the best in Canada. There is also excellent cross-country skiing in Labrador.

St. John's built many excellent sports facilities for the 1977 Canada Summer Games. For years, fans flocked to Newfoundland's Memorial Stadium to watch various sporting events, including the first-ever North American Ball Hockey Championships. In 2001, Mile One Centre replaced Memorial Stadium as the main venue for such events. The province has also hosted several gymnastic events.

**KEEP CONNECTED**
Get up-to-date information about sports in Newfoundland and Labrador at **www.nfsportsweekly.com**.

The Royal St. John's Regatta takes place on the Quidi Vidi Lake.

The oldest sporting event in North America is the Royal St. John's Regatta. This 2.6-kilometre, six-person rowing race has taken place on the first Wednesday of August since the 1820s. The carnival that accompanies the race is almost as important to the spectators as the race itself. Every year, more than 40,000 spectators attend the one-day Royal Regatta. The event is so popular that it is now an official municipal holiday. In 1901, a crew from Outer Cove set a race record for the St. John's Royal Regatta that was unbeaten until 1981. The crew are in the Canadian Sports Hall of Fame.

Deep-sea fishers dream of catching a giant bluefin tuna. They swim in Newfoundland waters, and some of them weigh up to 350 kilograms.

Newfoundland's air is supposed to be some of the freshest in the world. Tourist stores even sell it in cans, scented with fish flakes.

Corner Brook hosted the Canada Summer Games in 1999.

# CANADA

Canada is a vast nation, and each province and territory has its own unique features. This map shows important information about each of Canada's 10 provinces and three territories, including when they joined Confederation, their size, population, and capital city. For more information about Canada, visit **http://canada.gc.ca**.

## Alberta
**Entered Confederation:** 1905
**Capital:** Edmonton
**Area:** 661,848 sq km
**Population:** 3,632,483

## British Columbia
**Entered Confederation:** 1871
**Capital:** Victoria
**Area:** 944,735 sq km
**Population:** 4,419,974

## Manitoba
**Entered Confederation:** 1870
**Capital:** Winnipeg
**Area:** 647,797 sq km
**Population:** 1,213,815

## New Brunswick
**Entered Confederation:** 1867
**Capital:** Fredericton
**Area:** 72,908 sq km
**Population:** 748,319

## Newfoundland and Labrador
**Entered Confederation:** 1949
**Capital:** St. John's
**Area:** 405,212 sq km
**Population:** 508,990

## SYMBOLS OF NEWFOUNDLAND AND LABRADOR

FLAG     COAT OF ARMS     FLOWER
Pitcher Plant

Alert

Esmere Island

Baffin Bay

0 200 400 Kilometers

0 200 400 Miles

Baffin Island

Davis Strait

Iqaluit (Frobisher Bay)

Ivujivik

Labrador Sea

Hudson Bay

Schefferville

NEWFOUNDLAND

Happy Valley-Goose Bay

Chisasibi (Fort George)

Island of Newfoundland

Gander
Saint John's

QUEBEC

Sept-Iles

Gulf of St. Lawrence

St. Pierre and Miquelon (FRANCE)

Moosonee

Chibougamau

PRINCE EDWARD ISLAND

Sydney

Charlottetown

NEW BRUNSWICK

Fredericton

Quebec

Saint John

Halifax

Sherbrooke

NOVA SCOTIA

Montreal

Sudbury

Ottawa

Lake Huron

Toronto

Lake Ontario

Hamilton

London

Lake Erie

**BIRD**
**Puffin**

**TREE**
**Black Spruce**

**ANIMAL**
**Newfoundland dog**

## Northwest Territories
**Entered Confederation:** 1870
**Capital:** Yellowknife
**Area:** 1,346,106 sq km
**Population:** 42,940

## Nova Scotia
**Entered Confederation:** 1867
**Capital:** Halifax
**Area:** 55,284 sq km
**Population:** 939,531

## Nunavut
**Entered Confederation:** 1999
**Capital:** Iqaluit
**Area:** 2,093,190 sq km
**Population:** 531,556

## Ontario
**Entered Confederation:** 1867
**Capital:** Toronto
**Area:** 1,076,395 sq km
**Population:** 12,986,857

## Prince Edward Island
**Entered Confederation:** 1873
**Capital:** Charlottetown
**Area:** 5,660 sq km
**Population:** 140,402

## Quebec
**Entered Confederation:** 1867
**Capital:** Quebec City
**Area:** 1,542,056 sq km
**Population:** 7,782,561

## Saskatchewan
**Entered Confederation:** 1905
**Capital:** Regina
**Area:** 651,036 sq km
**Population:** 1,023,810

## Yukon
**Entered Confederation:** 1898
**Capital:** Whitehorse
**Area:** 482,443 sq km
**Population:** 33,442

# BRAIN TEASERS

Test your knowledge of Newfoundland and Labrador by trying to answer these boggling brain teasers!

**1 Multiple Choice**

What is the capital of Newfoundland and Labrador?
a) Gander
b) St. John's
c) Goose Bay
d) Stephenville

**2 Multiple Choice**

What is the provincial bird, the puffin, sometimes referred to as?
a) an ocean crane
b) a river buzzard
c) a sea parrot
d) a lake pigeon

**3 True or False?**

What percentage of the provinces land is farmed?
a) 1
b) 20
c) 80
d) 15

**4 True or False?**

The proper name of the province is Newfoundland and Labrador.

**5 True or False?**

Mummering is a form of ice fishing in Newfoundland and Labrador.

**6 Multiple Choice**

Which of the following is found off the coast of Newfoundland and Labrador?
a) oil
b) mining
c) forestry
d) fishing

**7 Multiple Choice**

Who were the first Europeans to explore the shores of Newfoundland?
a) British
b) Vikings
c) French
d) Swedes

**8 True or False?**

L'Anse aux Meadows is the earliest known European settlement in the New World.

1. B, The capital of Newfoundland and Labrador is St. John's.  2. C, The provincial bird, the puffin is sometimes referred to as a sea parrot.  3. A, Only 1 percent of the province's land is used for farming.  4. True  5. False, Mummering refers to the custom of actors and everyday people dressing up in costumes and performing traditional folk plays.  6. A, Oil is found off the coast of Newfoundland and Labrador.  7. B, The Vikings were the first Europeans to explore the shores of Newfoundland.  8. True

# MORE INFORMATION

## GLOSSARY

**admirals:** the leaders of fishing fleets

**bogs:** soft, wet areas of land

**Canadian Shield:** a region of ancient rock that encircles Hudson Bay and covers a large portion of Canada's mainland

**charter:** a written grant by a government

**Confederation:** the joining together of the Canadian provinces

**excavations:** digging up

**fjords:** long, deep, and narrow sea inlets formed by glaciers

**Gemini Award:** an award that is given for excellence in Canadian television

**hydroelectricity:** power produced by water power

**Moravian:** people belonging to a Protestant religion that was developed in Moravia and Bohemia in the Czech Republic

**mummering:** a Newfoundland tradition that involves wearing a disguise and parading through the streets

**Northwest Passage:** a route for ships travelling from the Atlantic to the Pacific

**tundra:** an Arctic or sub-arctic plain that remains frozen all year round

**wigwams:** dwellings that consist of cone-shaped frames covered with animal hides

## BOOKS

Beehag, Graham. *Canadian Industries: Fishing*. Calgary: Weigl Educational Publishers Limited, 2007.

Beckett, Harry. *Canada's Land and People: Newfoundland and Labrador*. Calgary: Weigl Educational Publishers Limited, 2008.

Koopmans, Carol. *Wonders of Canada: L'Anse Aux Meadows*. Calgary: Weigl Educational Publishers Limited, 2008.

Simon, Elizabeth. *Canadian Sites and Symbols: Newfoundland and Labrador*. Calgary: Weigl Educational Publishers Limited, 2004.

## WEBSITES

**Newfoundland and Labrador Heritage**
www.heritage.nf.ca

**Government of Newfoundland and Labrador**
www.gov.nf.ca

**Innu Nation**
www.innu.ca

Some websites stay current longer than others. To find information on Newfoundland and Labrador, use your Internet search engine to look up such topics as "St. John's," "Signal Hill," "Hibernia," or any other topic you want to research.

# INDEX